RADIOS

ALSO BY JEROME STERN

Making Shapely Fiction

Micro Fiction:
An Anthology of Really Short Stories (editor)

Florida Dreams (with Gary Monroe)

R A D I O S

Short Takes on Life and Culture

Jerome Stern

Drawings by the Author

W. W. NORTON & COMPANY

New York   London

For information about permission to reproduce selections from this book,
write to Permissions, W. W. Norton & Company, Inc., 500 Fifth Avenue,
New York, NY 10110.

The text of this book is composed in Bauer Bodini
with the display set in Bauer Bodini Bold Condensed
Composition by White River Publishing Services
Manufacturing by Quebecor, Fairfield
Book design by Susan Hood

Library of Congress Cataloging-in-Publication Data
Stern, Jerome (Jerome H.)
        Radios: short takes on life and culture / by Jerome Stern.
              p.   cm.
        ISBN 0-393-04119-0
        I. Title
     AC8.S753 1997
     081—dc21   96-40078
                                             CIP

W. W. Norton & Company, Inc., 500 Fifth Avenue, New York, N. Y. 10110
http://www.wwnorton.com

W. W. Norton & Company Ltd., 10 Coptic Street, London WC1A 1PU
1 2 3 4 5 6 7 8 9 0

for Bayard Stern

C O N T E N T S

Thanks are due to Ben Wilcox of WFSU-FM and Florida Public Radio, to Charlie Wade and M. J. Conboy, to Jane Greenhalgh of National Public Radio, and to Peter Breslau, Margaret Low Smith, and Laura Westley of National Public Radio. In addition, special thanks to Carol Houck Smith and Jesse Lee Kercheval.

A cassette version of *Radios* is available from the Florida State University Public Broadcast Center, 1600 Red Barber Plaza, Tallahassee, Florida, 32310, or by calling 1-800-829-8809.

As the family and many friends of Jerry Stern already know, he was a wearer of many hats. In addition to his roles as teacher, writer, scholar, and editor, he was an inveterate doodler. Over the years, his sometimes fanciful renditions of fellow humans and other creatures filled dozens of spiral-bound artists' notebooks. It seems fitting now to present a sampling of Jerry's doodles as a freewheeling accompaniment to his Radios .

RADIOS

LIBRARY

People tell me that they do not like libraries, they are too hushed, all those books make them nervous. I do not understand this. Libraries are wonderful places. Many of the things that happen to you in life are not so pleasant. Hardly any of these not so pleasant things happen to you in libraries.

When you are a child, people don't come up to you in libraries and say how you have grown and ask if you have been behaving yourself lately and have you done your homework and will you help to wash the dishes and did you write to your grandmother and have you cleaned out the catbox yet.

When you are in high school and in the library, people don't come by to see if they can beat you up or ask you if you still haven't gotten a job and if you made up your mind about what college to go to and if you learned the meaning of responsibility and who do you think you are.

When you are in college the library is even more wonderful because people don't drop in to tell you that you are spending too much money and not studying hard enough and never come home anymore and are losing all sense of decency and no one knows what's getting into you and have you decided on a major yet and who'd hire you with that.

And no one tells you that they never want to see you anymore and that you are the most selfish person they ever met and I don't know what it was but I don't think I ever really loved you.

And later and later the library grows more wonderful and becomes more beautiful and full and rewarding.

For people do not assault you in the library with overdue telephone bills and draft notices and subpoenas and bills of divorcement and dreadful phone calls that stop your heart.

And your car does not break down in the library and the washing machine does not die a howling death in the library and no one tells you of your manifold inadequacies as a member of the human race, how unfair you are, you really are, how selfish and insensitive and irresponsible, and that you never wrote to your grandmother and you still haven't cleaned out the catbox.

SUMMER CAMP

The summer I was twelve, I was sent to Camp Pine Cone. I was told I had a scholarship. Scholarship was the polite term at the time for charity case. I wove potholders without complaint and, when swimming, followed the rules about the buddy system.

After lunch, we were required to write letters. I dutifully did, to my parents, but the good ones were to my older brother. To enliven them, I concocted a camp inhabited by sadistic counselors and subnormal bunk mates and run by owners who were a cross between pod people and Nazi zombies. I liked to be imaginative about the food, pondering wildly on the source of the meats, and on the possible ingredients of the regularly served cold fruit soup, a purple liquid so strange to me I never let a drop of it near my mouth, so to this day I have no idea what it tasted like. The owners of Camp Pine Cone were actually a gruff, somber, and always anxious mother-and-son-pair, rarely seen except to warn us not to damage their canoes or stray into the woods. They were remote and stiff, like most adults.

In the middle of the summer, the owner, the son, came to my bunk and told me I was going home. He gave no reason. I was mildly surprised, since I was scheduled to stay, but I obediently packed, wondering if a paying child had been recruited to take my place.

I must have been taken to the station and put on a train. I got off in New York. I found the uptown subway, took it to my stop, and walked the several blocks home. I remember coming into the apartment and walking through some rooms looking for someone. My mother was leaning out the bedroom window hanging wet laundry on the clothesline. She turned and found me standing there. She looked unbelieving. The camp hadn't told her my summer was over. They hadn't told her they had sent me home.

Over the next several days, my parents found out what happened. The owners of Camp Pine Cone regularly opened the campers' letters. The lively portraits of the festering lake, the monstrous mosquitoes, and the satanic food apparently did not amuse the mother and son.

They told my family they had a right, even a duty, to read

the mail to make sure the campers were eating properly and enjoying themselves, that they violated no federal laws in steaming open the envelopes and even keeping offensive letters about the camp, since the letters were handed to the counselors rather than put in a U.S. Mail box, that they thought I was unhappy and wished to go home, that my parents were to be informed, of course, and there must have simply been some little mix-up. My brother had gotten none of my literary creations.

And I? I thought of them discovering the first disturbing letter. I thought of their annoyance. This outwardly cheerful if smart-alecky little boy so disrespectful, so ungrateful. But each letter was worse than the last. I could see them in their camp office at night, the steam kettle hissing away, their slipping my pages out of the envelope, hanging on my every word, growing more and more annoyed at my menu fantasies, my outrageous version of their Camp Pine Cone.

I imagined their waiting with impatience and anger to see what awful thing I might say next, their growing more indignant as the letters grew more vividly insulting, their sputtering and mumbling at a twelve-year-old's notion of wit. I thought of them unable to contain themselves in silence and with fury reading my passages aloud to each other. Oh, the power of the written word.

Will I ever have an audience like that again?

HEARING

I had a rusty cough that would not quit. I flew anyway to an academic conference to deliver my lecture on the psychosexual implications of the relationship of Mr. Ed, the talking horse, to Wilbur, his adoring owner. I rasped out my paper, showed some videotape selections to prove my point. I celebrated that evening.

The next morning my throat was aflame. I could not speak, I could not even whisper. I had gone silent. My larynx was a burning log. In the lobby of the hotel, I carried my notepad. I wrote to my friends, I CAN'T TALK.

My friends mouthed to me, HOW DO YOU FEEL?

I wrote, I CAN HEAR.

They said, YOU SHOULD GO HOME, and pointed vaguely east.

I wrote, COULD YOU TRY TO CHANGE MY RESERVATIONS FOR ME?

They bobbed their heads emphatically. They called, they explained, they convinced the airline.

Could I get to the flight?

I wrote, YES I THINK SO.

My friends wrote back, GO TO AIRPORT NOW.

I had my rental car. I got lost. I could ask directions, said my brain. No, I could not ask directions, said my throat. I found a likely street, and got lost again. I crossed lanes, I made illegal turns, I was running out of time. I got to the airport, but could not find where to return my rental car. I finally did. I jumped out. I waved desperately at an attendant and wrote on the rental car contract, I CAN HEAR BUT I CAN'T TALK. The guy zipped a return verification out of his hand-held computer. He kindly took my arm, waved the paper, and pointed to the office to show that I should take the paper in there. Inside stood a long, unmoving line. My forehead throbbed, my throat blazed. No one to help me.

A shuttle bus pulled up. I ran out, writing on my airline ticket, I NEED TO GET TO MY PLANE. I CAN HEAR BUT I CAN'T TALK. I tried to let my panicky eyes tell my story.

The bus driver looked at the ticket. She said nothing but bobbed her head affirmatively with much emphasis so I would understand her. She mouthed, SIT HERE. She zipped me to the terminal, pointed to the door, and waved me good luck.

I rushed to the desk to confirm. I wrote in my notebook, I

HAD MY RESERVATIONS CHANGED. I CAN HEAR BUT I CAN'T TALK. The guy smiled sympathetically and took my ticket. He silently pointed to the gate number.

The X-ray of my knapsack looked suspicious to the guard. They started to run it through again.

Aagh, I thought, it's the *Mr. Ed* tapes. If they run them through again they'll just be ghosts. I signaled frantically with my hands to say, "No, just look inside." I made a cutthroat gesture across my throat. I held up my notebook. They smiled understandingly and passed the pack to me.

I headed to my plane. I was touched by everyone's sympathy, their quick kindness, but I wondered, "Why won't anybody talk to me?"

REMAIN

Remain comfortably seated in the waiting area. Your seat number will be called. Your flight will be departing shortly.

Remain comfortably seated, for this trip may be your first or your last or one of the many trips you will take so

Remain comfortably seated. We are sorry, this flight has been sold out. Be patient. If you do not have a gate card, wait until those who have seat reservations have gone first so

Remain comfortably seated, as we will board in order of class and degree of foresight and quality of luggage as you

Remain comfortably seated, wondering if you will be allowed to be on this flight at all, or will you have to remain waiting, waiting for the next flight, and when will your life begin? And why are all those people ahead of you? And why are they smiling and laughing and kissing each other goodbye while you must

Remain comfortably seated. Your life will be starting shortly, your number will be called, and it would be better if you

Remain comfortably seated. Your cabin assistant will be waiting for you, a parent or parents or appropriate agency will be chosen for you,

Remain comfortably seated while your job possibilities are being discussed. The love of your life may be circling overhead. At some point a doctor will certainly be in attendance so you might as well

Remain comfortably seated. The other passengers seem certain this plane was made for them, while you wonder if this is your flight and if it is, will it take off smoothly? Will the weather be good? Will it arrive safely? Maybe it is better not to go at all, maybe on this flight you will not get to look out the window, the tray table will not go into its full upright position, the cabin attendants will run out of peanuts. And perhaps there is a better plane waiting in the sky that will soar and climb and have fine china and show you bright dawns and scarlet sunsets and hosts of golden daffodils and it is the plane that is meant for you that will take you beyond the horizon and into the land of your dreams and they are right after all, and you should

Remain comfortably seated.

FAINT

The summer evening air was thick enough to chew up and spit out. My head burned. My body was cold. Suddenly my head turned icy and my body got hot. I began to shiver and sweat at the same time. I was trying to be a delightful dinner guest, swirling my red wine, listening to a story about someone's erratic plumber. Perhaps I had not entirely recovered from my flu, perhaps I was too hasty in accepting this invitation, but I knew my hosts had gone to some trouble to fashion a pleasant evening. I was *expected*.

It occurred to me that if I fussed about the heat on the patio where we were laughing and eating guacamole I would interrupt the rhythm of pleasure we were building. Politeness gave me strength to hang on. When my feet went cold and my fingers got numb it occurred to me that I would be more comfortable in a cool tiled bathroom, perhaps to splash some water on my person, perhaps to bring my many body temperatures to a single harmonious chord.

I did not want to interrupt the beat of the conversation, now turning to the iniquity of prime-time television. I rose, excused myself politely, and headed into the house. But something happened. It dawned on me that I was not walking through rooms but lying on a floor. Perfectly relaxed.

It felt right to be on cool linoleum, but I was also looking up at our good hosts' sixteen-year-old daughter, who had been sent inside to see what had happened to me. She looked stricken. "Are you all right?" she asked this man whom she hardly knew, this prone friend of her parents.

"Sure," I said politely, getting up as if I customarily lay down in kitchens during dinner parties. "The bathroom is through this door? Yes?"

I found the shiny guest sink, rinsed my face, bathed my wrists, and came back out to the patio. The daughter, naturally, had reported finding me stretched out flat, spookily rising, and disappearing into the bathroom. The group did not quite know how to look at me. Tempo was endangered. I could see the problem before all of us. How to save the evening? The hosts had just served the pâté on toast points. Still to go were many foods, grilled meat, asparagus with hollandaise, chocolate mousse, cognac.

Politeness demanded that I insist that I was fine, that faint-ing away was just a thing I did from time to time. Politeness commanded the guests to studied nonchalance. Politeness told the hosts to hide their dismay. They offered me pâté. Politeness told me to munch enthusiastically to show I was still an eager eater. We must not be cut short.

Conversation rekindled. Glasses tinkled. My temperature stayed in one place. The shadow had passed, but I did not touch the cognac.

DOUBLE FEATURE

You're always worried about whether you're doing something wrong when you're raising your children,

Oh it's my fault she's so shy.

Oh it's my fault he doesn't do his homework.

I shouldn't have put on all that pressure.

I should have sent him to private school.

I didn't do enough positive parenting.

Forget it.

I've seen 'em come and I've seen 'em go.

Kids aren't young ducklings patterning themselves on your every waddle. Raising a child is not a complex interchange of psychological support and cultural education. You look back and you realize it's a much simpler thing. Raising a kid is just like watching a movie with an actor you can't take your eyes off. It's like an old Saturday matinee double feature—with coming attractions, cartoons, and war news.

You're the audience.

Your kids, the movie.

You yell things at the screen. Don't drive so fast! Don't try those pills! Can't you see that guy's a sleaze?

And if on the screen they slow down before they hit the fallen power line, avoid the creep, decide not to steal the car, you take credit. You say, "Lucky I was here to warn him. We've always had a good relationship." But if the kids onscreen get in trouble, you shake your head.

"I told you! Now listen!"

In the dark and scary parts you wonder why you came to this movie at all. "Wasn't this supposed to be an upbeat comedy?" you say to the person who brought you, if that person is still there.

You can even think, "I can't stand this!" and go out for popcorn, but you'll worry and feel guilty about what you're missing and scurry back, because, though you know it's a movie, you still gotta be there to say,

"Watch out. You can do it. Take care. I love you."

GO OUTSIDE

T he aunts and the uncles would sit in the living room talking. We children would hover at the edges. But our opinions on life were not sought. Instead, when we were noticed, someone usually said, Hey, why don't you kids go outside?

We would retreat into the hallway, shove each other, then slink back into the living room. It was not only that there was nowhere to go and nothing to do, but we felt we were missing the secrets of the adult world. How could they sit there endlessly, not doing anything, not playing anything, just talking?

We would filter back to behind armchairs, pretend we were deciding what to eat from the table, trying to stay inconspicuous so we could listen. What we'd hear was usually this:

How's Gloria doing?

Okay.

Okay? I heard she wasn't doing so okay.

She's doing okay now.

That's good, cause I heard she wasn't doing so okay.

That's over.

That's good. It never seemed such a great idea that she should get started.

Who can talk to her?

I'm glad everything's fine. And Phil?

Could be better, could be worse.

Yeah, who knows? A guy like him. Hey, why don't you kids go outside?

Outside there was a green lawn you were told not to play on. A backyard with thin grass. This was before anybody ever heard of four-hundred-dollar redwood swing sets. So we'd sidle back in and they'd still be talking:

Where's Leslie?

She said she wasn't feeling well.

So she's not coming?

She's been feeling bad all week.

I thought she'd be here.

She called.

She should see a doctor.

She goes to the doctor.

And so, what does the doctor say?

Doctors. They say this, they say that.

Hey, why don't you kids go outside?

We'd troop out for a little while but then we'd be back hoping to hear something, anything, that gave us some understanding of who those people in the living room really were, those people who loved us but would never say anything that made sense to us and who mainly wanted us to go outside.

DREAD

My pillow was wet from a night of chewing on one corner. Clammy little patches of dread had been migrating across my back for the past several hours. I got up in the darkness and pulled on my jeans, groped for a T-shirt and sweat socks, and quietly opened the bedroom door. I knew my shoes were out there under the coffee table. I laced up, patted my wallet, and smiled at last.

I was gonna be gone.

I went out the front door and looked up and down the dark street at the dark houses, the series of yellow bug lights over everybody's door.

Then I sort of flinched. Because I could see the street wasn't deserted. My next-door neighbor, Artie Webb, was outside too. He was just standing, like a man waiting for a train that he knows will never come. Then I suddenly noticed our buddy Jimbo, directly across the street, standing just the way I was, his right hand still on the door, pulling it closed, his body turned as if to take off from the house.

And in front of the place next to his, what looked at first like a shadow, there was Eddie Midger crouched down tying his shoes. In front of the other houses on the block I could see other guys, Doug, P.C., both in their driveways. And down the street I could make out this guy whose name I could never remember standing and holding what looks like a little suitcase or a thirteen-inch TV.

Slowly we are all noticing each other, and that we see each other, and have been seen by each other. It is too late to get back in the house, to pretend you were not there, that it never happened. Everyone had seen everyone. And we are all paralyzed from going further.

In that frozen moment we all, each of us, know why we are all out there, and we are seeing something in each other which we have denied in every hearty minute with each other, our daily "How are you doing, pal?"

"Just fine."

"Great."

"Wonderful."

"Terrific."

"Couldn't be better."

"Nyou?"

"Nyou?"

Because we have never, could never, acknowledge what we really know about each other from the confidences of our own wives, that we are nervous, we are depressed, we are frustrated at work, we are unpredictably irritable, we are suspiciously inattentive.

Now, how will we face each other tomorrow and say "Just fine," "Great," "Couldn't be better"?

It is a terrible, wonderful moment as we all stand immobile, looking at each other under the golden lights, and I hope we all move together in the middle of the street and form a circle, our arms on each other's shoulders, and sway back and forth as we slowly circle the hollow center of our individual losses and we will moan our woes like wolves and go back to our lairs trembling with relief and knowledge.

But suddenly somebody yells, "God! Did you all hear that too?"

That hangs in the air, and then there is a relieved babble of answers.

"Yeah, what was that?"

"Jeez."

"Woke me right up."

"I thought I saw a flash too."

"God."

We all shake our heads with comradely astonishment at the mysteries of the universe, and turn back to our own houses, so we can lie down once more, and wait for the light.

READING THE
REFRIGERATOR

The scratchy crunch of a muffin or the chewy mouthfeel of a bagel? Which do I want? Maybe I'm not hungry at all? If I look here long enough I'll know. I stand at the open refrigerator meditating, just as I did as a child when I was nose level to the second shelf. We used to call it reading the refrigerator.

Early in the morning I would find my sister staring as if hypnotized, her face bright in the white light of the refrigerator bulb. She'd be eying the carton of eggs and I could see in her mind—Soft-boiled? Sunny side up? Scrambled, yes, if there was rye bread, and the rye was toasted, and the dish with the daisy design was clean. If not, just white toast. With strawberry jam. If there was any strawberry jam.

Our younger brother, whose head was one shelf lower and who couldn't even make a peanut butter sandwich, would pull open the door and stand in the cold. He would look deep into the wilting celery and softening carrots believing that if he waited long enough he could stare a box of Mallomars into sudden existence.

We would all get told to shut the door and stop wasting electricity, but I believe reading the refrigerator started with my father, a meditative humorous man who loved to eat whatever horrified us most. Calves' brains and lambs' kidneys. Scaly fishes cooked in broths that in the refrigerator turned to green jellies pierced with tiny bones like shark fins. Cheeses so pungent we assumed his liking them was some sort of complex trick.

He too would contemplate the bowl with yesterday's spaghetti, the leftover pot roast, the sprouting potatoes. His brow furrowed, he would peer for all of us, for our coming supper.

Twenty years after he died, my mother told me she woke up one night. There was a light in the kitchen, and so she went down the hall. It was so real, she felt as if she could talk to him. He was simply standing there, she said, quietly reading the refrigerator.

DESSERT

The main course has been cleared away. The four of us at the table sigh with satisfaction and self-celebration at going to a real restaurant with real tablecloths. The waitress approaches. She has been polite and professional. She described the main-course specials with authority and nodded affirmatively with each choice, as if to recognize our remarkable good judgment. She has served with efficient calm.

But now, as she comes to our table, her face is different. She looks at us coyly. She is smiling as if she knows some amusing secret about us all. She is beguiling, seductive. "What can I tempt you with," she says, and rolls the dessert cart before us. She describes each torte and mousse shamelessly, her tongue lingering over words like "raspberry" and "eclair." "Whipped cream," she says, and I wonder why we aren't all arrested.

This has nothing to do with sex, though. It is the special moment of sinfulness at these restaurant meals—it is the moment on the edge of dessert, the dizzying point when dietary aspirations dance dangerously with forbidden pleasures. It is a solemn and giddy ritual, tantalizing in its subtlety, its moments of suspense.

Each diner is engaged in a deep private negotiation: Do I need it? No. Do I deserve it? Yes. Do I deserve it more than I don't need it? Maybe. What are the others doing? If no one orders dessert, I'll look like a glutton if I do. If everyone else orders a dessert and I don't, I'll look like a spoilsport, a wimp, a prude.

We all eye each other. It can go either way. The reckless friend who daringly points to the Napoleon will be followed by giggles of group naughtiness and eager choosing of Black Forest cakes and mocha puffs.

Or someone will decisively say, "None for me," and the table will dutifully follow suit, mumbling its noes, and feeling the vitality drain from the evening. Our celebration, our momentum, lost to caloric piety.

But more often than not, in these days of negotiated pleasures, something else happens. Eyes meet across the table, desire and denial intermingle, there is a delicate pause, and then, "Who will share that crushed almond chocolate log with me?" and a taker agrees at once. The strawberry cheesecake quivers with acceptance. "And four forks," someone says as if it were a very clever thing to think of. Festivity returns, and we are a party of happy children, as the Cleopatra of the dessert cart smiles and moves on.

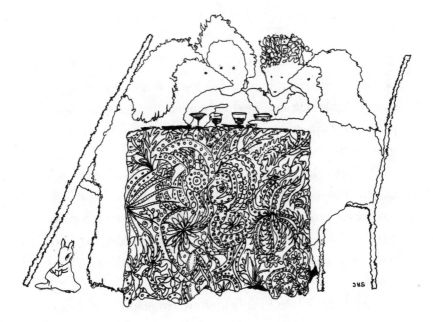

DOCTOR

I am losing weight, I notice. But losing weight is good in our society, a blessing bestowed only upon the deserving. I eat pâtés, pasta, pastries, but harmlessly. Perhaps it is because I walk so quickly, leap up the stairs, talk so much.

But I also have fevers, persistent night sweats, a flu that will not flee. I guess my heat is causing my weight loss, a metabolic furnace cooking away excess calories. The night sweats feel like going to some midnight spa, waking up soaking wet but strangely elated. But the condition seems curious, even worrisome.

I go to the doctor. I tell him of my symptoms, my physiological adventures, this odd trip my body has taken. You don't look well, he says.

I agree.

You look gray, he says.

Well, thin, yes, no one has quite said gray.

The doctor looks gloomy. You don't look well, he repeats. He looks at his chart. You've lost a lot of weight.

Yes, I know that.

Night sweats? he says.

Yes, as I had already told him.

I'll send you for a blood test now, he says. And for a CAT scan tomorrow.

No flu, no virus, no quick antibiotic fix, something serious, deadly serious, the word that cannot be uttered. I can deal with that, I think. I'm a fatalist, a man of a generation that knows how to face bad news stoically. I ask a few intelligent questions about chronic infections. It is probably a malignancy, he says without warning. His face says "fatal."

I faint, passing out into a dream of dreaming. This makes me feel wonderful, but must alarm the doctor. He and his assistant have to haul me into a chair. He is relieved when I return to consciousness and is ready to hospitalize me at once. He prefers conversations to melodrama.

People are supposed to get examined, get advice and prescriptions, not drop to the floor in these tiny rooms with their sunflower wallpaper. As far as I can tell he looks worse than I do. He is happier with healthy patients, curable ailments, predictable conditions.

I find myself assuring him that I am fine, in control. I totter out of his office to begin my days of testing. I have the feeling I am beginning a new life, however short it might be.

MAD

So I don't know, I don't know what the teacher wants from us. I mean, the teacher gives us these notes on John Milton and then he asks us if we have any questions and we can't have any questions because we don't know what to ask and so we are quiet and then he gets mad at us.

And then he asks us if we heard of Jean Paul Sartre and Reinhold Niebuhr who we never heard of and are not on the syllabus, and then he gets mad at us for not having heard of people no one ever told us about.

And then he says what about *Crime and Punishment* and *War and Peace?* which it turns out are books that nobody even ever mentioned in our lives, and then he gets mad at us.

And then he gives us things to read which are very sad and confusing and then he gets mad at us because we don't like things that are sad and confusing.

Then he says life doesn't have happy endings and we say why does it have to be that way and that's why we want to read things that have happy endings and then he gets mad at us.

And we tell him we would do what we are supposed to, but he won't tell us what we are supposed to do.

Think, he says, think, why don't you think. And then, when we tell him what we think is that we don't understand what he is saying, and what will be on the exam, and will we be responsible for everything in the syllabus or just what we cover in class, then he gets mad at us, and says all we care about is grades and money.

And then he gets sarcastic and asks us when World War II was, and then he gets unhappy because we don't know, and never heard of Mussolini or Mao or Molotov cocktails, and we don't know why we should have heard of those things so there doesn't seem to be any reason to know these things.

And then he gets mad at us and says all we care about is ourselves and we don't even know who we are, and that is not the way it was at some time before, but what that time was is not clear.

We do not know that time because it was a time maybe before we were born, and he seems mad at us because we were not born when he was, and did not do the things he said he did, and that it is all our fault.

He does not like what we like and is mad at us for liking the things we do like instead of other things which no one ever told us about, and so he is almost always mad, but we hope he likes us and gives us good grades anyway.

GAME

My fingers dance on the keyboard and my eyes stare intensely and my brain cells sizzle and fry. I am playing a computer game. It is a copy that someone in the office gave me that he got from someone in the next building who got it from her friend who heard about it on e-mail and downloaded it from a bulletin board and said this one was total hypnotic excellence and you can never quit playing it once you have started.

I didn't want it. I said no, I was busy. I have better things to do. But like the drug pushers in the TV public interest announcements, he cajoled and bullied and guilt-provoked, and so I said, Okay, I'll see what the excitement is about, and now I can't stop and I should either go cold turkey or send the evil geniuses who write it their blood money for devising this malevolent thief of time.

I have to keep the door of my office locked because students think I am in here diligently reading their papers and writing perceptive and thoughtful comments, and my friends think I am in here writing brilliant critical essays, and my wife thinks I am in here working my fingers to the bone dealing with nervous agitated undergraduates who want to know what grade they will get for their stories about throwing up in backyards after drinking bouts in which they mix vodka and beer and Southern Comfort—stories that not only have the squalor of authenticity but also catch the sense of waste I have come to know so well.

This hopelessly pointless game is slurping up thousands of life-seconds like a voracious anteater in a giant colony. My fingers dance on buttons and I can feel my time on earth being shortened, my vitality being sucked, my head spinning. I am using these fragile moments of our brief vanishing years, these precious minutes of lucidity that crumble sooner than we think, not to answer human correspondence, not to record my thoughts, not to do good in the world, but to press cd: GAME. GAME, and squawk goes the screen and little figures bounce out, pointlessly jump, and more moments of my life gasp like guppies and flop over gone and I can't help it. I can't stop.

If I finish a game, I stare at my score for a moment and I do not press EXIT, I press PLAY. The phone rings. Why are people calling my office? What do they want from me? I don't know anything. I have no answers. Why don't they leave me alone?

Do I know the secrets of literature? The meaning of art? The schedule for next term? How could I? I am busy devouring my own brief time, chewing it up, spitting it out. Good score, better score, worse score, my neck hurts, my eyes swim, another try, just one more, my desk is covered with papers, the phone is ringing, I have a meeting I am supposed to go to. I will in a minute. . . .

MORNING NEWS

Iget bad news in the morning and faint. Lying on the tile, I think about death and see the tombstone my wife and I saw twenty years ago in the hilly colonial cemetery in North Carolina: *Peace at Last.* I wonder, where is fear? The doctor, embarrassed, picks me up off the floor and I stagger to my car. What do people do next?

I pick up my wife. I look at my wife. I think how much harder it would be for me if she were this sick. I remember the folk tale, that once seemed so strange to me, of the peasant wife beating her dying husband for abandoning her. For years, people have speculated on what they would do if they only had a week, a month, a year to live. Feast or fast? I feel a failure of imagination. I should want something fantastic—a final meal atop the Eiffel Tower. Maybe I missed something not being brought up in a religion that would haunt me now with an operatic final confrontation between good and evil—I try to imagine myself a Puritan fearful of damnation, a saint awaiting glory.

But I have never been able to take seriously my earnestly mystical students, their belief that they are headed to join distant ringing spheres. So my wife and I drive to the giant discount warehouse. We sit on the floor like children and, in five minutes, pick out the largest television set in the whole God damn store.

LOOKING FOR
MR. KEATS

I was just beginning to take courses in literature, and I was in search of absolute ideas. Professor Gravepepper walked into the room and held up a mimeographed copy of Keats's "Ode on a Grecian Urn," which I'd just read, the poem that says, "Beauty is truth, truth beauty."

"Where is this poem?" Professor Gravepepper said unexpectedly.

"In your hand, sir," one of the front-row people said.

Professor Gravepepper crumpled up the sheet and rimshot it into the green can against the wall. "Where is it now?"

"In the wastebasket," a student said.

"So John Keats's great poem 'Ode on a Grecian Urn' is in

a wastebasket in room 318," He made it sound as if that couldn't be right.

"Well, *your copy* is," the guy who sat behind me said sarcastically.

"Aha!" said the professor.

I figured I caught on and leapt in before anyone else could. " 'Ode on a Grecian Urn' is still in our books. We *all* have 'Ode on a Grecian Urn.' "

"We all have *copies*," the back-row guy said snidely. I did not like him.

Gravepepper seemed to enjoy this. "So do you have the poem or a copy of the poem?" He didn't wait for an answer. "Where is it? In the British Museum? Is Keats's manuscript the poem, or is that just Keats's copy? We came to class today to study John Keats's 'Ode on a Grecian Urn' and I want to know where it is."

I was puzzled. If "Ode on a Grecian Urn" is not on the paper it's printed on, then it must be somewhere else. If it's somewhere else, then it wasn't here. But I had it right here.

Gravepepper ran on. "If you burned every copy, would it be gone? What if someone still had it memorized? What if that person died?"

I thought maybe there could be some sort of poetry heaven. But I wasn't prepared to raise my hand and propose the idea of poetry heaven to the class.

The professor looked pensive. "So how can you study it if you don't know where it is?" he said. "If you burn 'Ode on a

Grecian Urn,' or the Theory of Relativity, or the Declaration of Independence, what exactly have you destroyed? Something? Nothing? It? Yourself?"

I looked toward the wastebasket for an answer. My head hurt. What did all this mean? When was Gravepepper going to explain about beauty and truth and how that's all ye know on earth and all ye need to know? When would I find out where ideas really are?

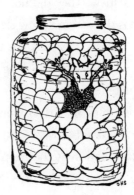

CLOSETS

I am at a party. Everyone is better dressed than I am. The hosts are giving a tour of their home. They love it, they say. It is brand-new. They did not want to buy a used house.

He is dressed in yellow slacks and shiny brown loafers with leather tassels. His shirt has tiny golf clubs. She is wearing an ivory silk blouse and a long gauzy skirt. Puce, she tells me. They take us upstairs.

Everything here is strange to me. First the front door of the house is a handsomely lacquered garage, as if the cars owned the place and kept the people as pets. Then the living-room ceiling soars several stories up with high windows, as if the guests were occasionally giraffes.

One wall is taken up with a huge television screen sur-
rounded by worshipful smaller electronics—all twitching with
glowing blips of light. Tall speakers stand like sentinels in each
corner. Symphonic versions of the theme music from famous
television programs of the past are being played. The only furniture I see is a tiny couch and a round glass coffee table.

We all go to their bedroom. It is small and over their garage.
She opens a door to show us a larger room. It has rose-color
lighting and the smell of sachet. On every wall, skirts, blouses,
slacks, and jackets beautifully hang like iridescent waterfalls.
Fuzzy sweaters snuggle against each other. Bright summer
dresses party together. Her suits are meeting to discuss policy
issues. No longer stuffed in drawers or crammed in closets, I
can see that these clothes believe this is only what they deserve.

The husband is eager for the tour to continue. That isn't all,
he says, and opens another door to show that his clothes have
a room of their own. Rows of slacks hang evenly, each with its
own breathing space. Shirts not only all face in the same direction but are organized by color, whites shading to pastels, pastels brightening to primary colors, then darkening to earth
tones. Florals and stripes have their own rack. Jackets and suits
have their own wall. Behind a louvered door he shows us a
roomful of his boots, shoes, and slippers holding a leathery conference of their own.

We go out into the narrow hallway. Isn't this place wonderful? they say. We have to show you the linen closet. You could
live in it.

WALK

My short-haired, thick-bodied brindle dog asks me for a Christmas walk.

I say to him no, it is too cold.

He points out the advantages of me taking him out right now versus the disadvantages of waiting too long. I point out to him the disadvantages of discomposing me, and his becoming friendless during the holiday season.

He agrees but points out that any diminution of affection will be noticed by our visitors, who will then think considerably less of me. His belief is that he is the true attraction of the household, and it is for his sake that my friends tolerate me.

I take his point and his leash, and he takes me and his walk.

It goes like this often, these discussions.

We walk downtown to look at the lights. I point out to him that white lights have come into fashion, and that is a contrast to the lights I knew as a child. He points out to me the fascinating odors that lie at the juncture of sidewalks and curbs.

I urge him to look up and think about the difficulty of stringing bulbs so high and handsomely. He is busy nosing a particularly complex manhole cover.

I tug sharply on the leash to capture his attention.

He looks up and agrees that the white lights are festive indeed and that he sees them as fresher than the dark greens and blues and reds of old-fashioned lights which always remind him of lonely roadside motels.

I take his point and draw him toward the great, decorated, cheerfully communal holiday tree.

We agree that the tree is brilliant and splendid and democratically inclusive.

I urge him to appreciate the ingenious blinking electric star at the top.

He is inclined toward a close examination of its lower branches.

I celebrate the bubbling glass candle decorations reminding me of past trees I've known.

He, remembering my calling those very same ornaments, on another occasion, dribble sticks, accuses me of false nostalgia, a self-indulgence of which he disapproves.

When we pass a display in front of a church with its life-size manger, we fall back into agreement about its impressive realism, but while I want to meditate about transcending sectarian differences and the meaning of the wise men for all humanity he lowers his sturdy body, digs in his paws, and strains mightily toward the fragrant straw under the kneeling shepherds.

So we leave quickly and hurry home to his bone biscuit and my hot cider and so good night for our merry Christmas.

CAT SCAN

I am at the radiologists for this thing called a CAT scan. The nurse gives me a green sheet with three dining-plate-size holes along one edge and points me to a cubicle. I take off my clothes. I am not sure what to do with the sheet but try to figure it out.

It seems logical to me that two holes would be for my arms and the middle one for my head. I try that. It leaves a loose flap of cloth which I surmise must be gathered togalike in one hand, and my head pokes out crookedly. Bad design? Maybe one size doesn't fit all.

The nurse looks at my disarray. No, she says, and rearranges the holes so I have one hole for one arm, curiously two holes for the other arm, and the head magically free.

Better. She gives me a gigantic plastic cup of a chalky-looking malted to drink. She cheerfully explains that she'll be back every fifteen minutes with more cupsful for the next hour.

I am skinny and shivering. The nurse sits me on a green plastic bench and smilingly explains that the machines like it cold. I understand that the machines' needs are greater than my own. They live here. I am just passing through.

I obediently drink, shiver, drink. I talk to a thin lady who joins me on the bench. She is having her brain scanned due to bad headaches. I am going to get a picture of my pelvis since I am losing weight and have been feverish. I am called into the room of the pampered machines.

I am moved to the bed of the machine, connected to an IV, have odd things done to my lower anatomy, and then the nurses, who have been cheerful and friendly, leave the room.

I lie back. Alone. I feel soothed. The beige arc of machinery that I am moved under has a logo like a new car called something like Cybex 2000. It has a digital display in crisp red numbers. I hear a voice. It is the computer. The computer talks to me. "Breathe. Hold your breath," it says. Then it whirs and clicks. I close my eyes, not wanting to see whatever is going on around me. "Breathe. Hold your breath. Breathe. Hold your breath."

I am trying to breathe and hold my breath but I am losing track of which is which. Breathe, I have to tell myself, means not to hold my breath, it means to take a breath. "Hold your breath," the machine says, but now I'm out of the rhythm and

I need to take a breath. I hold my breath not wanting to disappoint it. "You're breathing," it might say, "when I am telling you not to."

I want to please the machine. I don't want to fail its expectations. I am back in synch. The whine and hum of the machine is quieting. The nurses come back in to detach me. I am glad to be released but a little disappointed. I want the machine to say, "Fine breathing and holding your breath. You've done a very nice job."

It's that magic hope that being good will save me.

CAT

Our father was rubbing the cat's head, her back, her neck. "Hmm," he said, and his fingers stopped. "There's something here." He pulled back Sonja's fur, and uncovered a scabby little ridge around her neck. He scratched at it with his fingernail. He got tweezers and alcohol from the medicine cabinet, took Sonja to the window for better light. She stayed very still, her head stretched out. He finally dangled in the tweezers a thin strand matted with bits of fur. "It looks like a rubber band," he said sadly. "Who put a rubber band around the cat's neck?"

We children looked around darkly. We knew we had played What shape can I make her tail? We remembered the game Can a bobby pin hold her ears together? the experiment How long will a cat stay upside down?

But we all loved Sonja dearly, and felt terrible and turned on each other with despair and guilt. We relentlessly repeated the haunting question "Who put the rubber band around the cat's neck?" No one admitted anything. We chanted in our beds, "Who put the rubber band around the cat's neck?" We'd whisper it over and over at breakfast and late at night, teasing each other, waiting for someone to admit to the awful deed.

But I wondered, Had I? It was true I had put the cat in galoshes. How could I be sure it wasn't me, careless, forgetful, cruel.

We chanted and tortured each other for weeks, for months, and I writhed with self-doubt. Sweet Sonja, however, recovered quickly, and was forever after treated as a hero, fed chopped raw liver, coddled, and years later went to the home of all the great wonder cats.

After many more years, no longer children and living far apart, at a family gathering I announced that I was the one. "No," my sister said. "I did it."

"No," insisted my little brother. "It was me."

"No," said my elder, "I remember."

We argued all over again. Each had personally constructed his own vivid memory of the incident, had harbored her own private shame.

"We all did it," I finally offered, thinking of the ever-patient Sonja. "Even if we didn't do it, we did it."

We all knew what I meant. The issue was settled. Far-flung

as we were, we remained a family, bound by our histories, whatever we thought they were. What guilt has brought together no facts can tear asunder.

PHILOSOPHY

The first day in philosophy the professor somberly taught us Plato. It seemed reasonable to me. We were all shadows of an ideal that only existed as an abstraction. Chairs could only be imperfect copies of the wonderful, absolute idea of chair.

Then we moved on and I was sure that Aristotle was right. What we can see and touch and measure is reality. What could an ideal be but a fabrication made from what we already had? If we had never walked in forests, how could we imagine the notion of trees?

We left behind Plato and Aristotle and jumped into Hume and Berkeley and Locke and Kant. The professor seemed to find all these systems faulty but I liked each new idea as fast as it appeared. The world existed. No, it didn't. Trust your senses. Your senses lie. God exists. No, he doesn't. Each one was persuasive. Each one was true. Language constructed reality. Reality constructed language. I think therefore I am. I am therefore I think.

The professor sadly continued to explain their various fallacies. But I loved them all. Existence precedes essence. Essence precedes existence. Life is meaningful. Life is absurd.

The students in the class were fierce. They kept saying that whatever anyone else said was wrong. They shouted to each other, "Define your terms."

The teacher morosely pointed out their argument was based on the idea of meaning, and meaning was impossible.

That's good, I thought, then there's nothing to argue about. I wanted to tell them to like each other. "Don't you see, you're all right!"

But that didn't seem to be the point. Someone had to be wrong for someone else to be right. "Totally illogical!" a guy yelled, and others snickered in triumph.

Logic was just another unprovable idea, the teacher unhappily explained. That sounded great to me. I was right to believe everything all at once.

But the class seemed upset. "Then why are we here? What's the point?" they cried.

"Perhaps it's all a dream," I offered to no one in particular, since they were all too intense to pay attention to my tentative mumble.

"Who'd dream this?" said a voice behind me, and I turned to find a dark-haired girl with her head down doing the *Times* crossword. She looked up and flashed large, dark brown eyes. Eyes that said we should be elsewhere, drinking coffee, finishing this puzzle.

Ah, Truth at last.

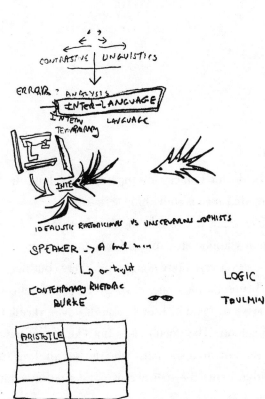

MARROW

The doctor's office calls me. Come see him, the nurse says.
I know that means something serious.

It does. The doctor tells me they have found a mass of some
sort in my abdomen. A mass. I take to the word at once. Some
sort of secret ceremony going on in there. But not a good one.
A dark mischievous one, a congregation of selfish cells. But
maybe we can end it, I think, shut it down, shrink this sinister
congregation. The doctor does not like giving news like this.
He'll send me to a specialist who deals with these mysteries.

Within hours the specialist is pondering my chart. I've lost
weight, lost color, feel weak, I must seem a thin gray sheet, a
crumpled tent, a shadow. The doctor is interested in taking a

sample of my bone marrow. He asks if I would like to schedule that. He says he can do it right in his office. He could do it now if I wanted. "Some patients want to think it over, or wait a day or two," he says. I don't believe I have a day or two.

"Right now would be good," I say.

I lie on the examining table, my head on a silly little pillow. Do people take naps on these? I wonder. The two technical assistants who prepare the equipment are happily girlish. One shows the other how to roll out sterile needles from their envelopes so they drop on sterile pads instead of rolling on the table. It looks like they are unwrapping utensils for a cupcake recipe. They giggle a lot as they unpack each part and see if they can do it right. I am thinking my fate is in the hands of children.

The doctor comes in when they tell him. It seems still like a game, ready or not here I come. He has me roll over on my side. My head is on the little pillow. He pushes the needle into what feels like the back of my hip. I feel a stab, a shove, but it's a shove that is not on the outside but on my inside, within my flesh, against my bone. And then a little more, a little harder. I discover I'm not a screamer, a wriggler, a yowler. I'm silent, but I'm biting down on the little pillow like a cowboy on his bandanna as he is getting a bullet extracted by the light of the campfire while outlaws circle in the darkness.

The doctor says, "Just hang on a little more." Another poke, another thick shove. It's done. My jaws unclench. It's not severe pain, I realize. It's like when you're at a party and animatedly acting out a story and accidentally back into the corner of a marble table. Ummph, you'd say. Ouch. An ouch, a soreness, a bruise, and that's about it.

It's not really pain. Pain is waiting four days to find out what it means.

STILL, LIFE

I said to her, "Listen, art is better than life. Cleaner, purer, more significantly arranged."

She said, "But it isn't real."

"It is more real," I said, "Reading about fishing is much better than fishing. Reading about traveling is more satisfying than traveling. Looking at a painting of a bowl of fruit is more interesting than looking at a bowl of fruit."

"But how can you say that?" she said.

"Ten hours in a boat is claustrophobic, uncomfortable, smelly, and boring," I said. "Guys tell crude jokes. They get cranky when things aren't going just right. They make lame excuses for dumb mistakes. Time passes slowly. But Hemingway makes fishing beautiful, comradely, a sacred ritual."

She said, "But I want to see things for myself."

"It takes too long, you miss too much. F. Scott Fitzgerald puts a lifetime in your hands. You can see more of the South by reading William Faulkner for one hour than by driving around it for twenty years."

"It's crazy. Art can't replace life," she said,

"Crazy, that's another thing," I said. "If you have a nervous breakdown you cause misery to your family, tens of thousands of dollars in medical fees, and it takes years to recover. But if you read Kafka you can experience madness and just close the book."

"It just doesn't make sense," she said. "We're alive. We have to live in this world. We have to make a living."

"That's so we can afford to go to museums and read books and listen to music."

She said, "Why not go out and enjoy life itself. Smell the flowers. Look at the birds."

"That's not what people do in life. In life they mow lawns and pay bills and sponge the mildew off their furniture."

"That's not all there is to life," she said, "There's parties and conversations and good times with friends."

"Most people," I said, "are secretly uncomfortable at parties, have heard all the conversations many times before, and are chronically irritated with their good friends."

"But what about me?" she said.

"What about you?"

"I mean what about us?" she said.

"About us?"

"What about when we share a chocolate mousse? Isn't that life? What about love? Isn't that life?"

"No, that's not life. That's art," I said.

"That makes no sense," she said.

"That's life," I said.

THE TASTE
OF LIFE

Your mouth is a sensual sea. A Godiva has just begun to break open inside it and the apricot creme is beginning to ooze from its chocolate structure. Your mouth doesn't know whether to hold intensely still so that the chocolate walls will slowly collapse or whether you should let yourself crush the chocolate with your teeth and squish out the creme. The slightest of movements and the sweetness rushes you into a momentary rapture which passes into a peaceful sigh. You have been chocolated.

Science does not know this yet, but these calories can do you no harm. These are the calories of life, the calories which nourish the soul, enrich the psyche, let you transcend the daily round at the mill with slaves. These are not the dangerous empty calories of nutritionists' nightmares. Empty calories are empty of thought, attention, concentration. Empty calories are those mushy wads people stuff in their mouths while they are arguing about the lawn. Empty calories cause obesity.

Full calories are the delicious moments of your autobiography. The Sacher torte at the hotel in Vienna, the ice cream soda at Rumpelmayer's, the French chocolate cake that made you cry because every bite you took meant one less bite to take.

Full calories are Mozart symphonies, redolent, orchestrated, perfect. These calories, these voluptuous calories, can only make you beautiful.

BOXES

"**A** college boy," they'd say, "and you don't know how to tie a decent knot?"

Over the roar of diesels and honking horns, they could yell directions to a truck driver backing his semi into a loading dock with only six inches of clearance on each side. They could turn corrugated cardboard into giant boxes like magicians spinning out handkerchiefs. And all the while they could keep up their deadly comments on my ignorance, my ineptitude, my inability to understand the simplest instructions.

"You call this three feet of tape? This is enough to gag my Aunt Hattie."

"You don't know how to get back from Avenue C? Drop bread crumbs."

If I interrupted a conversation to ask a question I got yelled at. "Can't you see we're talking here? Don't they teach you manners in college?"

If I waited politely, one would suddenly turn to me and say loudly, "You practicing to be a statue? What? What?"

If I talked in a regular voice, they'd shout, "Speak up. We ain't at a tea party."

If I yelled, they'd tell me, "Talk normal. Nobody around here is deaf."

I kept thinking of brilliant and withering comments that I dared not say. "I'm sorry, sir, my university doesn't offer a course called Use of the Tape Dispenser 101." I had childish fantasies of suddenly becoming enormously wealthy, appearing in my limousine, buying the business, and firing them all.

They kept expressing disbelief that a college boy could not keep their orders for sandwiches straight, that a college boy didn't know where to sign a delivery receipt, that a college boy was unable to follow orders in plain English like "Put all that stuff for later all in the back and stack up what we're gonna need now so we can get to it, and throw out the rest."

I made it through the summer and a couple of them did notice I was leaving and said touching things like "Watch out. I hear them coeds bite." The guy who ran the paper baler said, "Don't flunk out, college boy, or you'll wind up back here with us," laughed, and waved his three-fingered hand at me.

Jerks, I thought, I'd drown myself first.

In the middle of winter sitting in a classroom, I remembered the time the guys heard me humming and for the rest of the week called me Dr. Warblemeister. I had to admit it. I missed the loading dock. Those guys had turned nasty jobs into a kind of ongoing performance art in which they were both the actors and the audience.

During this incomprehensible lecture on political science theory I finally realized what those guys were telling me about social reality. So I did learn something in college after all.

WAITING

The doctor extracts a morsel of my bone marrow on a Thursday. Call Monday, he says.

Yeah, call Monday to find out if carcinogenic cells are crowding my bones like subway passengers at rush hour.

Noon would be a good time, he says.

I lie in bed at night watching myself get thinner. Touching ribs and hipbones. Rubbing my tibia and fibula, wondering what's inside them. It hurts to sit in a chair. The feeling is not only that I'm getting thinner but also shrinking, becoming filmier, elfin.

I get thinner all weekend, losing what feels like a pound a day. After three weeks at this rate where will I be? I have lost what we call appetite. Hunger has just gone away. But I still know what to do. Put food in front of me. Fork by fork, pick it up, chew slowly, swallow, repeat. Plate is empty.

I curl up on the pink sofa watching television. Watch movies, talk shows, Barney, Ronco food dehydrators, CBS news at four a.m. pretending it's an ordinary daytime show. No reference to night owls, the inverted lives of nocturnal America—insomniacs, nightshift workers, patients with unidentified diseases. Straight daytime-style coverage at four a.m. Makes life seem normal. Thousands of us in our pink sofas, our house trailers, rollaway beds. What else should we be doing but watching a story about miniature goats when the dark night of the soul stalks the land?

Monday morning. Today is the day. Waiting for Monday noon. I'm in fine shape, I tell myself, working on not thinking about what I'm not thinking about. At eleven a.m. I watch *Charley's Angels*. Charley's Angels are in trouble with a kidnap plot involving an ambitious roller rink owner. One Angel has to go undercover as a dancing skater to figure out what's going on.

Noon arrives. I wait a careful five minutes. I call the doctor's office. I am perfectly calm, I tell myself, just an inquiry, just wanting to get the results of a test. I say who I am. I am put through. I reintroduce myself.

The doctor is direct. "No cancer cells are showing. Nothing in the marrow," he says. "It looks clear."

I don't shout with elation. I discover I can't even talk. My throat closes. My voice creaks. I make a thumbs-up sign to my waiting wife. She doesn't know Roman arena symbology so looks totally puzzled for a moment. Those days of tension ignored, evaded, denied, now choke me.

I thank the doctor. He carefully adds that there could be problems elsewhere, but it's clear that this is a reprieve. I can barely breathe. Good news can be as scary as bad news. I'm teary-eyed. I thank him again in a whispery voice.

"Next thing to schedule," he says, "is a biopsy in the hospital. Get out a sample. See what that mass means. They can do it in a few days. You'll check in in the morning, be out by the afternoon."

I'm looking forward to it. I realize I'm glad they think I'm worth the trouble.

I C E

When I was little, our freezer hung like a little mailbox inside our refrigerator. It was just big enough for an ice tray and a box of frozen peas. The tray sat congealed in this tiny prison in a thick white iceberg. Getting ice out meant reaching in, getting my fingers stuck on frozen gray aluminum, and scraping my knuckles as I edged the tray through the hole in the glacier.

The ice was yellow-gray and solid as rock. I'd bang the tray against the sink, pour water on the bottom, pry a block loose, try to catch it in midair before it crashed to the drain. I'd wash off each lump and sink them into my warm soda, never enough to really chill it.

Then my father brought home a tray with a lever on top like

a jack handle. The lever was supposed to spring the blocks of ice loose. The ice groaned, wheezed, squealed, and I'd end up with this jack handle hanging on to the tray with all the ice blocks still stuck together. So once again I'd take it over to the sink and turn on the hot water, failing once more to catch the chunks and fragments plummeting to the dingy porcelain. The pieces I rescued would have an unhealthy bloom of frost on them, like a white fungus. In they'd go, foaming ominously in my glass.

Then came the plastic tray. You just twisted the tray and all the cubes, they said, would neatly pop out. But they didn't neatly pop out, and they weren't cubes. They were pebbles and they'd suddenly explode loose and skitter across the floor.

When I was ten we were all invited to a cousin's fancy wedding. They had liquor for the adults and sodas for the children. The ice cubes were as clear as crystal, as smooth as glass, as sharp as dice. They tinkled, they laughed, they spoke of a life I did not know. And thought I'd never know. These people probably also had matched living-room sets and china knickknacks. Rich people, I decided, had perfect ice.

And so today, when I finish looking at my students' papers, bicycle home from work, open my modest freezer, and see my little icemaker, happily filling its little ice basket, I cannot think how inefficient, how impractical, how wasteful it might be. I can only think how happy I am, how quietly content. At last, at last, I have perfect ice.

EARLY START

An early start, they say, go to bed early because we are going to get an early start. I put the rods and the crab nets next to the door and wake up at dawn. They get up at nine.

They say they want coffee, the dog has to be fed, the cat has to be fed, do I have all my stuff together. They look grim and edgy. I can't find my left flipper. The sunscreen has gone gummy. The ice chest smells bad.

Now they say they are hungry, everybody should eat something first. Where is my tackle box? Nobody can find the big pile of beach towels that was just washed yesterday. Now they are scrambling eggs. The tackle box must be at V. J.'s house. I can't wash the smell out of the ice chest. They say they might as well fry some bacon too.

On the phone V.J. says he doesn't have the tackle box and I might have left it on the porch. They decide the ice chest always smelled that way. I find the tackle box on the porch sitting on top of my left flipper. They say sit down and eat, all this food is not going to waste.

We sit down, and they start reading sections of the newspaper. V.J. comes over to help me look for the tackle box I already found. He starts to go through it for old stuff that might be his. They start putting sandwiches in the ice chest. We are told to start loading the car. We find the beach towels in the laundry bag. We forgot we put them in last night. The cat gets in the car.

They decide they are not going to just leave all those dishes in the sink all day. The cat comes out of the car, but then gets underneath it. We load the rods so they stick out the back window. The dishes get washed. The cat comes out from under the car.

Everything's ready. What did they forget? Nothing. They just have to stop to cash a check, buy some gas, check the oil, get ice, pick up sunscreen, and drop off a key. Then we will be on our way. They are smiling now.

They tell each other how great it is that we all got off to an early start.

BIOPSY

I am lying in a crisp little hospital bed waiting for my turn to have a biopsy. The CAT scan has found a mass lurking in my abdomen. We are all puzzled by its origin and composition but know it's not a good thing. It bodes badly.

The nurse is of the new tradition. She tells me what she is doing and why. She takes my pulse, my temperature, my blood pressure, and my blood. She asks me if I'm comfortable. She explains that I'll be taken downstairs in less than an hour. I'll have some sort of dreamy anesthetic so I won't feel a thing, she says. She again asks me if I am comfortable.

I am, I tell her, and it's true. The sheets are crisp and the bed is firm. It's on wheels, she shows me. I won't have to move a muscle.

A large man shows up. His badge says transportation aide. He threads the bed out of the room. We work through the hall traffic, passing, weaving, changing lanes. A medical interstate highway of nurses moving in convoys and doctors gliding by like expensive sedans. I look at the world through my feet. We descend in an elevator full of stout people with stethoscopes.

I get wheeled out into a dim, quiet corridor. No families with flowers and balloons. No candy stripers. It seems to be a hallway of abandoned mobile beds. A sort of garage. But I see the shapes of feet. I realize each bed has a supine person covered, like me, by a white sheet. There's a long line of beds spaced apart like planes waiting for an open runway.

At intervals a door swings open and the bed goes into motion, taking off into a world that will explore the mysteries within the passenger. You bought the ticket but not the route. The flight but not the destination.

A door opens up and a guy signals the waiting stretcher bed in front of me to sail into the next room. I get a smile and a thumbs-up saying my time is coming.

Then my door opens and I get to go. I expect something austere like the *Star Trek* control room. But what I see looks like a ham radio shack piled high with electronic gadgets, blipping and wiggling tiny screens, a giant yellow machine crammed to the ceiling, and a crowd of people so thick I think of a circus clown car. Hardly seems room for me in this party, but I'm supposed to be the honored guest.

Hands grab different parts of me, and each person is simultaneously explaining, wrapping something around me, and holding up clipboards so I can give my permitting autograph, and I'm already floating off on some sort of ether waving goodbye.

I awaken, landed in the quiet hallway. They have delved deeply through my skin, my muscle, my body wall, like petrological engineers, drilling for cores, and extracting a sample of the mysterious mass, the alien retroperitoneal ceremony. What I have to show for this massive exploration of my inner darkness is a tiny Band-Aid you would put on a mosquito bite.

The transportation aide takes me back to my room. I doze happily until the nurse comes in and asks me if I'm comfortable.

I am. I don't know what will happen next, but I'm comfortable.

When the whole family would assemble for an occasion, the kids would flock around my Uncle Victor. "Why do you hang around him?" Aunt Fern would say, puzzled. She didn't understand the appeal of his stream of anecdotes, always with a funny slant, about outrageous coworkers, unfair policemen, and crooked politicians. The other uncles were serious, solemn, carefully noncommittal; everything was always going fine.

We'd rush to Victor for his grousing criticism of the party. "Look at these little plates. These are for dolls to eat off. What are we, a family of midgets? You can't get a roll on these plates." He'd advise us, go for the roast beef. "Don't be fooled by the potato salad."

He'd point out aunts who were too fat, too thin, too talkative, too snooty. "She doesn't have time to say hello to me," he'd fake-whisper. "I'm not good enough. Not like her husband the hat manufacturer."

We loved him. He'd talk to us. The rest of the family, everything was below the surface, a matter of shrugs and nods, single words that stood for ancient unspoken grievances.

He'd get up. "Enough of this stuffing my face with this food I don't need. Let's take a walk." And we'd all follow him out of the stuffy house and, as he would say, "inspect the neighborhood."

He'd comment derisively on the fat shiny cars in the driveways, the rigid green front lawns, the pompous bricked-in mailboxes, the bronze nameplates, Dr. James Waruga, Ph.D. He taught us the word "redundant." "A million-dollar word. You should learn a new word every day," he told us.

And every once in a while he'd approve of something. It was always unpredictable. A plastic chicken on a front lawn. "There's someone telling the neighbors where to get off," he told us. Or he'd admire what looked to us like a battered old sedan. "Someone loves that thing," he'd say admiringly. "You ever see a Hudson before?"

And then after a while, he'd turn around, "Back to the Heart of Darkness my friends," and make a miserable-looking face that made us laugh.

It took years to figure out what he did to us. How he communicated to us a kind of irritated pleasure in our relatives.

Sure, some were tiresome, but they were yours: you came, you greeted, you groused. You were kind to the elderly, you saw through the fancy talk.

Victor's grouchiness was a form of celebration of whatever life hands you. He was teaching us not to be overly impressed by what money can buy, but how to be a person: think for yourself, keep your sense of humor, and learn a new word every day.

He was teaching us, you wanna have a good time, hang out with the kids.

PRIVACY

I am watching the new *Newlywed Game*. The host has just asked the wives to tell what their husbands will say when the husbands are asked what article of clothing is most likely to make their husbands say "Va va voom."

We already know how long they knew each other before they first made whoopie. The couples joyfully betray each other for outdoor barbecue sets. I think of them selling their most private acts, their personal intimacy, to the audience, which is laughing at their crossed stories and public squabbles.

"You don't remember that time in the kitchen?" The audience whoops with salacious delight.

These people are clowns, with no sense of shame, no sense

of privacy, of middle-class dignity. I sink deeper into my depression at their eagerness to tell the world whether on their first date she was as slow as molasses or easy as pie. This is the ultimate in American tastelessness.

Then I begin to realize something. These are not the people who have been fooled into believing that their lives are insulated by two-acre lawns and uniformed doormen. The new newlyweds know that from elementary school on they've been measured and quantified, that in order to get their jobs, what jobs they have, they have been credit-checked, background-checked, and foreground-checked.

And they live lives of urine tests and blood tests and lie detector tests and school transcripts and police records and intimate questionnaires, and they have to give their social security numbers to anyone who asks them or go without what they want. Every purchase they've ever charged, every blouse and jacket and motel bill, is on the computer. Their medication, their polyps, their bladder, their anxieties and depressions are all recorded as permanently as their dental X-rays.

And should anyone believe they are of any significance, their neighbors will be questioned, their family investigated, and their old friends quizzed. And the new newlyweds know this and manifest their lack of privacy with liveliness and vigor. And their exhibitionism defies taste and dignity, and redeems them.

The new newlyweds know they've been tagged, they've been bagged, they've been itemized, they've been inventoried, they've been weighed, they've been assayed, and they've been betrayed, and the only aspects of their lives that they control they control by saying it first. *What we give, you can't take.*

These people are not fools, for they understand the present and they foretell the future. The new newlyweds act out our reality. It is not a game. It is prophecy.

The only difference between us and you is that we're getting an outdoor barbecue.

C L U E

I talk to the doctor. The results of my biopsy are peculiar. My mass is definitely unfriendly, in fact, malignant. But what sort is unclear. Morsels of me will be sent across the country to specialized laboratories for closer readings.

I like the idea, these slides and reports, traveling about, being examined by experts while my fever and I stay home lying on the pink couch. It is an odd form of tourism. Yes, I can tell my friends, I've been to San Diego, well, not exactly all of me. The doctor sounds like a detective, deducing, narrowing down the list of possible perpetrators. As I listen I think about playing the game of Clue. I remember that the victim's name was Mr. Boddy. Who had attacked him? Professor Plum in the

Lounge with a Wrench? Something, somehow, is doing me in, I think, and I wonder how long I can go around the board before the villain is caught.

I am learning words I don't even like to think, much less say out loud. Members of the cancer family whose names make up a scary rhyme that goes, Lymphoma, carcinoma, sarcoma, melanoma.

The doctor sifts the evidence. Despite conflicting clues, my symptoms draw him to a conclusion. He accuses lymphoma. He is our Colonel Mustard in the Hall with a Knife.

The treatment would be chemotherapy. I imagine a laboratory, pots of boiling flasks, ferocious-looking medical devices, steaming liquids. But I can't help looking forward to it. Action at last. The guns will be turned in the other direction.

Fill these prescriptions, he says. Take them in the morning. Show up here early tomorrow.

I get up and chew on toasted waffles so I can swallow my pills, get driven to the doctor's office. I feel so weak that walking up the dozen stairs tires me. I've lost a couple more pounds.

I'm shown into a bright little room with a child's picture on the wall. The nurse is friendly, smiling, chatty. She seats me in a green BarcaLounger. I look away from what is happening to my arm. I look back down and find that she has put an IV on my wrist faster than I could have buttoned a cuff on a dress shirt.

I look away again as she inserts syringes into my IV, and we talk about weather, schools, dogs, and if I want to kick back another notch on the lounger. She says I might feel warm, or sleepy, or something could sting a bit. I feel all right. As she works we talk about traffic, parking, and malls. And then she says we are done.

I go home wobbly, I sleep, wake, and sleep. In the morning I take my temperature with my peeping digital thermometer. I stare at the number. Not 102.1. 97.6. No fever. My forehead is cool.

It could be coincidence, it could be ephemeral, but something makes me believe the right suspect has been arrested.

GLASSES

When I was a freshman in college, the words in my textbooks began to get fuzzy. Movies started to look as if they had all been shot in soft focus. Streetlights wiggled at night as if they were underwater.

Our neighborhood optometrist, who had a green neon sign in the shape of spectacles, put me in his chair, showed me eye charts, and told me to come back in a week for my glasses. I picked out black plastic frames that to me looked forcefully intellectual. I put them on and it seemed that print grew sharper, that road signs grew clearer.

I wore them in graduate school so I could study night and day. I never really liked them much. If I wore them when I ate, the food seemed on the other side of a glass wall. No one ever told me I looked intellectual.

After a year or two, traffic lights were again dancing in the dusk. I decided I needed a stronger pair for my tiring eyes. The university health plan entitled me to a real ophthalmologist. He had dilating fluids, tiny lights, spinning prisms, a dazzling array of ocular splendors that sent my eye into orbits they had never seen.

He held my black-framed glasses in his hand. He spoke to me with authority. "You shouldn't really use these glasses anymore," he said. "You don't want them."

Just as I feared, I thought.

"You don't need stronger glasses," he went on. "You don't need any glasses at all."

I left the office puzzled. Who was right? I remember it was a bright, blue day. I looked up. The air was transparent. I realized from the upper branches of black oak trees individual leaves were waving their spiky tips at me. Pine needles glistened. I realized I could read crosswalk signs three blocks away. My whole body felt different, elastic, energetic.

I opened the little anthology of metaphysical poetry I'd carried into the waiting room. The letters of a Henry Vaughan poem stood crisply on the white page. I felt silly and strange and wonderful. What had happened? What were my eyes doing for the last few years? What had I talked myself into? It was as if the doctor had told me that a mistake had been made on my birth certificate and I was five years younger than I thought. I was the same person but a different person. I felt lighter, more supple, more vigorous. I breathed fresh new laughter.

He had broken through my invented weakness. I felt the power of the laying on of hands, of the magic of healing, of shamans, priests, witches, doctors, of medicine men, root women, conjurers, curanderos, of the history of medicine, the mysteries of organisms, of millennia of curing people, of potions and powers, of the subjective nature of reality, the restoration of the spirit, the power of the mind.

My heart sang out, "I can see, I can see." I leaped over a low fence and headed into my new world of light.

CELEBRITY

The morning interviewer says to Meryl Streep, "What does Meryl Streep think about being famous?"

Meryl Streep answers, "Meryl Streep resents her loss of privacy." Meryl Streep speaks as if she is talking about another person.

The evening interviewer asks what a Robert Redford feels when he reads the morning paper.

"A Robert Redford does not like what is happening in the world," Robert Redford says. He has become a Robert Redford, as if his fame had made him split like a stock or explode like a supernova into a great many Robert Redfords. Julius Caesar did it too. Julius Caesar would tell his interviewers what rivers Caesar would cross when Caesar came to them.

Today we learn what makes a Michael Tyson angry, what a Dustin Hoffman misses most, what a Mick Jagger thinks about in his middle years. What ever happened to I, Me, My, Mine?

We have risen to recognize that personality is too complex for a simple I. We look at the selves we've fabricated. We are splintered mirrors reflecting a thousand possible surfaces. Egos have swelled so enormously that we have grown too large for our pronouns. The celebrities have shown us the way. But a Robert Fabnudge is irritated by people pulling in front of him in traffic as much as a Bill Cosby. A Rita Parsnip has problems finding a good dry cleaner as severe as a Rita Coolidge. Let's make this a populist movement.

Someone asks you a question, forget the feeble I, the outdated I, the falsely unitary I. Speak out and say, "A Stuart Warfle sees the trees being cut, and it makes him sad." Be forthright with your loved ones: "A Francis Zimini doesn't like to come downstairs and find his eggs cold."

Answer with authority: "When an Angela Varnish makes breakfast she expects people not to dawdle in the bathroom."

We owe this to ourselves. We're as good, we're as complicated, we're as important. These celebrities, they have fame, fortune—should they have all the proper nouns too?

In naming ourselves we create ourselves, we are the stars of our own sweet universe.

GOLDFISH

·

I am arriving for my third chemotherapy. The nurse who has
been running my treatments, a brilliantly warm and efficient
woman, told me she would be away, that a substitute would
administer the IV. I am doing better with every treatment,
gaining weight, but am still fragile, easy to spook.

The new nurse calls me in. She is quick-moving and quick-
talking. She sits me in the lounger and I lean it back. A man is
complaining about government interference on her boom box.
She is talking on the intercom phone as she takes a sample of
my blood. I am hoping for her undivided attention. She wants
to save time. I want to save me.

To set up the IV drip she searches for a usable vein in my

wrist. She sticks and a little swelling gathers around the needle. Oops, she says, that one won't work. She feels for another place, stabs, tapes the needle in place, and I am ready

As she works she chats, she tells about how the family needs more room and so they weren't going to get the kids another dog since they might be moving into an apartment while they were getting the house sold before they found the house that they wanted, and so no dog for them now, but the dog they did have they had for ten years but then it started to have heart problems, and so they put it to sleep because it would cost too much to keep him alive.

She is changing from pushing an orange chemical into my vein to attaching me to an IV drip of something green.

Then she got the kids goldfish, and her daughter named them Bob and Milly, and Bob did okay but the next day Milly turned up dead. So she put Milly in a freezer bag and kept it until she could get back to the store and get a new goldfish. The man in the store said you never could tell how long a goldfish will live and sold her another goldfish. That one got named Milly too, so they had Bob and Milly again, and Bob was all right, but the next day Milly's fin was looking all funny, and so she went back to the store, and the man told her it could have been fin rot and there was medicine for it. She wasn't going to spend a lot of money on medicine for an eighty-nine-cent goldfish but it turned out to be a dollar or so, so she decided to try to cure her daughter's goldfish.

She begins to detach the snaky tubes from my arm and goes on.

So I came back to the house and I got a syringe and measured out the fin-rot medicine real exactly and put it in Milly's bowl. Well, the next morning, there's Milly dead in the water. Well, my daughter said she didn't want another goldfish because they die right away.

She pastes a bandage to my wrist and smiles. You're all done.

I push down the footrest of the lounger and stand up.

Good luck, she says brightly.

SCENE

I am walking into this crowded cafeteria right behind Bernard, a guy I probably knew since the second grade and occasionally hung out with even in college, but we hadn't been in touch for years till we bumped into each other on the street and he said let's have lunch.

I thought about what an energetic guy he was, and I can't remember exactly why we drifted apart. He always had something going. In the fourth grade he sold firecrackers, in high school he forged hall passes.

In college he got himself a huge motorcycle and a black leather jacket. He'd talk about Ayn Rand and tell me he could get me stereo equipment very, very cheap. Then I heard he went to law school, and sure enough, here he is in a three-piece and thin socks.

There is a long line of people waiting to get to the food. "Follow me," he says. In his prosperous lawyer suit he strides past everybody. I tag along. He stops at the front of the line, gracefully sidesteps ahead of a medium-looking guy with his face in neutral. The guy sees that Bernard is not passing through but is taking a tray as if he has all the right in the world. I take a tray too.

The guy jerks awake and says to Bernard, "What do you think you're doin'? We're all on line here." The guy can only imagine that Bernard doesn't understand cafeteria life.

Bernard turns. His whole body goes suddenly rigid and quivering as if he's electrocuted. His eyes turn crazy. He opens his mouth so you can see all his teeth at once and he spits out:

"WHAT'S THE MATTER? DO YOU WANT TO MAKE A SCENE?"

The man freezes. He reads about this sort of thing in his newspaper every morning, he sees it every night on the six-o'clock news. He is a normal guy waiting to eat his chicken à la king and go home that night to watch television with his wife and children. The man says, "No. No. Go right ahead!"

Bernard gives an epileptic shudder, as if he's managing to shake off a homicidal seizure, and starts choosing a salad. The guy picks up a tray, grateful to be alive.

I am remembering why I stopped hanging around with Bernard.

DOODLERS

In elementary school, down the margins of papers that should have been filled with problems in addition and subtraction we blackened in rows of meaningless boxes and chains of endless curlicues. The teachers would yell when they caught us. "No doodling on your papers," they'd say. "Your books are for your work. I don't want any doodlers in my room."

There were others in the class, the gifted children who could draw real-looking horses with complicated saddles, golden retrievers pointing at birds, men with chiseled features, and beautiful women with heart-shaped faces and long graceful legs.

The teachers loved them and gave them huge sheets of

paper to create homages to Arbor Day and Open School Week. They were taught the color chart, and supplied with long brushes and jars of poster paints. They drew orange pumpkins and brown turkeys, and their posters were hung in the hallways. "These are my artists," the teachers would say and point them out to admiring visitors.

We doodlers stayed in the margins with our ballpoint pens, hardening our style into angry spiked thickets and obsessively depressing checkerboards. The sixth grade and already our fate was sealed. We would never have anything wonderful to show the world. We were the doodlers, the unchosen. Our works destined for paper napkins, the backs of envelopes, the edges of our lives.

In the seventh grade we met our new art teacher, a Mr. Brine. A sour, quiet man who growled at the whole class. He said he wasn't interested in who could do the jolliest Santa. He didn't care about lettering. He seemed to dislike everyone equally. Mr. Brine wanted us to draw fish.

But not the fish we had for dinner, he said. He wanted fish with flippers like the wings of eagles, fish with colors nature never heard of, fish with jaws no evolution could create. He told us the color chart was the prison of art.

Those who could draw the perfect faces were puzzled. Staying within the lines seemed to mean nothing to Mr. Brine. We doodlers, rejected by all, slammed color all over the paper. We drew with fistfuls of crayons. He told us we were wonderful. We exploded fins into lightning bolts. He said we were full of energy. Our fish shimmered like Byzantine mosaics, roared like thunder gods. He held our work up to the class. Look, he'd say, look, these fish are like comets, they shine like stars. This is drawing.

Oh, Mr. Brine, we were doodlers no more. You gave us fish and the fish did make us free.

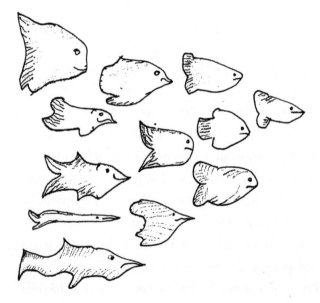

SYMPATHY

I get letters reflecting on life and its vicissitudes. Printed cards with pictures of geraniums or teddy bears in a straw basket. People worried about the inadequacy of their words. They fear platitudes. They wish they had some original idea to offer.

But I—the hesitant one, for my whole life so uncomfortable about expressing either condolences or concern to the bereaved or afflicted for fear of being shallow, mundane, clichéd—I read every expression of care with gratitude. Judgment, criticism, evaluation, never crosses my mind. Anything that means *I'm thinking of you* cheers me immensely. I want solace, not genius. Wit is its own reward, but a hug is as good as a sonnet. A blessing as sweet as a symphony. There ain't no trite in my world of fright.

I think about how often I had planned on buying a card, writing a note, addressing an envelope, finding a stamp, getting it in the mail. How often I had thought of that but not done it. I'd explain to myself why it might not even be right to do, that it could an intrusion, maybe even an irritation.

I'd seen those movies when the sensitive bereaved soul is outraged at the conventional expressions of sympathy coming from what seems to him the complacent community. "Smug in their luck!" he shouts. "False pity in their hearts!"

Doesn't hit me that way when my chicken is in the pan.

GRASS

I am looking for the address of my friends in a new condominium complex baking in the hot sun. The sign says that it is devoted to luxurious living in tropical ease for today's now people. The ground all around it has been bulldozed, graded, and paved in squares of grass that are supposed to settle down and root and make a green lawn. The squares have been flung down by the builders of luxurious living in tropical ease for today's now people so that the pieces of grass are partly on top of each other, and others have flopped over so they are smothering themselves. The ones that are supposed to be the edge of the lawn lie halfway out on the concrete sidewalks. They look like they are trying to escape and find a better place to grow up.

"Don't do it," I tell them. "You won't make it out there. You'll dry out."

They think they can inch their way back to fertile meadows and gentle rains, and be able to live in peace. I drop to one knee and try to explain to them that they need roots, they need earth, they need to be attached. I figure if I can move a few around I can slide some back and save their lives. But they are heavy and soft and now they are all trying to move, trying to find some way to live, and they start to make small frightened noises like grass makes when it is threatened.

"All right, you guys," I say. "There's gonna be room for you, air, water, everything's gonna be all right."

But it's not easy. I get down on my knees on the lawn and try to give them the chance they should have had. I have one in my hand and I'm looking for a place for him when my friends come out of their unit.

"Hi. Hi," they say, "We saw you from our solarium."

"Hi," I say. "I just noticed your sod looked pretty unhappy."

"Oh yeah," Heather says. "It needs to rain."

"It looked to me like they were trying to get away," I say.

"Ha ha," they say. "Come in and have a drink."

"Don't worry," I say quietly to the square in my hand, "I'll fix you up later," and I put him down gently.

"S'go man," Darryl says. "We got the AC cranked up and a blenderful of banana daiquiris going begging."

"Yeah," I say, "right," and stand up in the dying grass.

BLOOD

I roll up my sleeve to have my blood drawn from my arm. Lately I've been thinking of myself as a small boatload of people, a slightly feverish mind commanding and quizzing a torpid crew—Need a nap? Time to get moving! You'd better eat something now!

The phlebotomist draws two fat vials of rich red blood and takes them into another room. I wait for a few minutes as the blood is given to a sensitive and intelligent machine. Within minutes it knows more about my blood than I ever can. It counts my platelets, measures my hemoglobin, tolls my cells both red and white, calculates my hematocrit and I don't even know what hematocrit is.

The machine spews a little paper shaped like a cash receipt from the supermarket. It says I'm anemic. Not enough iron to keep this ship sailing happily. White blood cells are on the borderline of despondency. Red blood cells are undernourished. The whole crew is wobbly.

I take my readings home and ponder them. I don't want to wallow in these dark seas. I need to encourage this gang, to rally them from the bridge, get them to pull together. I remind my blood about the importance of cooperation. I need plump little cells. Tiny barges loaded with iron ore. Lively swarms of eager corpuscles.

Let's talk, I tell them. Mutual interest. We always liked each other. When I scraped my elbows you made terrific, crusty scabs. When I sliced my knee your anticlotting guys grabbed your proclotting mates quick and slowed the flow of blood until I could get stitched up. You toted great gobs of oxygen around so I could keep running happily in multikilometer races with my heavy-breathing hypercompetitive companions. You kept my brain enriched through late-night study sessions as I tried to grasp the permutations of geological millennia.

I've led you faithfully through storms and seas. I didn't fill you with a lot of smoky poisons, make you carry heavy loads of lards and lipids, I cut back on the french fries, exiled omelets. Remember friendship. Remember loyalty. Let's set the sails, start bubbling with vitality, loading some iron, preening our platelets, sweet-talking our bone marrow out of its indolence.

We aren't on different sides here. We're pals, allies, working together for our mutual benefit. I'll give you what you want, sleep, applause, support. Let's do the right thing. Surprise the bright lagoons, give the sunrise a new name, ring in the new year. Go onward. Blood buddies, blood brothers, we're in this for each other.

HOBBY

J eanette Camphezi made camels and hippopotamuses out of colored pipe cleaners. William Bile collected stamps from New Guinea and Tanna Tuva. Billy McGore, who lived over a garage, carried a shoe box of baseball cards which he had mostly won from little kids. Stanley something or other, whose father was a waiter downtown, brought in ashtrays with names of famous nightclubs.

We brought our collections to school. We'd lay out our miniature trucks and our impaled insects in glassine boxes on tables in the gymnasium and everyone from the first grade to the sixth would file by and stare at our treasures with envy and derision. Teachers said we all had to have something in the show. And so Dennis Zatch entered his catcher's mitt, and said he oiled it every day. Gerald Kizeer had snuck letter openers from his father's desk and claimed them as his own.

It was called the school hobby show. Grown-ups used to ask you what was your hobby. And you were thought of as a bit dull-witted if you didn't have an answer even if it was kind of lame, like saying, "Helping take care of my little sister." A hobby was what you made or collected or liked. It was something that took time. Sports didn't count as a hobby; that was something you just did. My hobby was cutting out pictures of cars and airplanes from magazines and pasting them in a scrapbook that was held together by a big shoelace.

It changed the way we knew each other. Denny, whose tales of home life were full of fighting uncles and broken furniture, revealed his boxed sets of hand-painted French Grenadiers and mounted Hungarian Hussars. Helen, who was too shy to speak a word in class, laid out white handkerchiefs embroidered with perfect tiny bright flowers.

Our hobbies were private, mysterious. We didn't know why we felt happy taking apart radios or collecting bottle caps. It was not as if we could remember why we *wanted* to record daily barometric pressures like Jay or to make linoleum-block leaf prints like Johanna. We didn't *decide* to read about horses or to keep a terrarium.

It was more magical than that. We dimly realized even then, walking around that echoing gymnasium, that what we loved had really chosen us.

ROTISSERIE

No home could be without one, we were told. Everyone was getting them. I was puzzled. We already had an oven in the stove.

No, I didn't understand, it's so much trouble to turn on the gas and ovens take forever to heat up and make the whole kitchen hot and get dirty and are hard to clean with dangerous chemicals but the electric countertop rotisserie oven was clean and chrome and modern and everything made in it would taste good and you could watch things cook through the glass and know when everything was done perfectly and it had a motor-ized spit which automatically would rotate chickens and they would roast beautifully in their own juices so Mother wouldn't have to baste constantly and burn herself and spend all her time slaving over a hot stove trying to make dinner because it would all be rotating slowly by itself in the delicious red glow of the clean heat and she would have more time to play with the children and you could bake cakes in it so easily because you could see when they were done and your friends could come over for cupcakes anytime because it wouldn't be any trouble.

And the chickens will glisten like red honey with crispy skin and the lamb chops won't be strange and gray and we'll have steaks seared with stripes like in the restaurants and everybody will be healthy because all the fat will always be dripping off everything and we'll all be feeling better and playing outside a lot after dinner because nobody will be tired from slaving over a hot stove all day 'cause cooking will be fun, with the little motor turning the barbecued chickens and watching the glass door and admiring the shining dial with the different colors for the different heats and the badminton net's set up and nobody's bickering about anybody sitting in somebody else's place and we will always be like a picnic.

X - R A Y

I am lying on a narrow table looking up at a sculpted beige device called a simulator. Red laser lights crisscross my body. A white-coated radiation dosologist calculates power levels. A computer printer sketches a shape to be re-created on me. I am a color-coded readout.

A nurse outlines rectangular blobs on my belly and my side with a slender blue pen whose brand name is the Personalizer. These will be the targets of the rays of radiation therapy. I like the idea of being radioactive, shining in the dark like the tiny luminescent green snowman I played with under the covers long ago, like the shooting sparks in our atomic ring toys, like my feet in the shoestore fluoroscopes we would stand in to see our toebones.

I am taken from the simulator to the real thing, the Mevatron. My first impression is—it's a hair dryer ten feet high. My mass will get the ultimate permanent wave. Chromosomes will become addled. When they try to multiply, the malignant cells will deliriously dissolve.

I lie on the table as the Mevatron's giant head swings above me. Perhaps not a hair dryer, but the mouthpiece of a giant telephone. I'd like to speak to it, ask what a Meva is, but I must remain still. The lights dim as lasers line up my blue marks exactly. The Mevatron will thread its invisible rays between vital organs to strike my alien invader.

The cheerful nurses turn the fluorescent ceiling lights back on and tell me all is ready. Then they leave. They'll be right back, they say.

My moment at last, alone, center stage, waiting. I'm a bit disappointed that the room doesn't remain dark with a couple of baby spotlights for dramatic effect.

I am wondering what the Mevatron will sound like. A deep throbbing, a low hum, a high whine? It is quiet, then a noise that I recognize, an uneven buzzing—it is the sizzling crackle of a patio bug zapper.

I count. One mississippi. Two mississippi. About a twenty-two-second buzz. Silence for a few moments. The electrons ricochet all over the room and into oblivion.

The nurses come back in. The giant head rotates like a robot arm, swinging under me and aiming up through the small of my back. I stare at the acoustic tile in the ceiling. One nurse dips beneath the table to make an adjustment. She bobs back up. Peek-a-boo. They look satisfied at me and flee the room. The zapper buzzes again. They come back in. The robot arm swings around to aim at my left side. The nurses align and again escape. The Mevatron zaps once more.

The nurses return. They smile at our mutual adventure. Tomorrow I will return, tomorrow, and tomorrow and tomorrow. Twenty-seven zaps, I am told.

And then?

And then, I'm told, we'll see.

BUTTER KNIFE

When we needed a tool we children headed straight for the kitchen drawer. We'd dig through wooden mousetraps, splintered clothespins, nests of lamp cords, clumps of string, and one-toothed electric plugs.

What we wanted was a dull gray slab of a knife. Though it had a handle as heavy as rock and a blade like an automobile spring, we called it a butter knife, but if it was a butter knife it was for a table service for Vikings. We'd yell when we found it like the problem was already solved, each of us grabbing to be the wielder of the mighty instrument.

If a window was stuck we'd wedge its blade between the

frame and the sill, chipping at paint and warped wood. We'd shove and slide and wiggle. After a while, with a creak and a groan, up the window would go. We'd cheer at our victory and the butter knife would go back to its drawer.

When skate wheels got wobbly or a doorknob spun around, we'd head for the butter knife, our ultimate and only screwdriver to deal with whatever mysteriously loosened itself, no size too small, no angle too difficult.

It pried bike tires off rims, spread glue in scrapbooks, and opened packages from the post office. It stripped wire and separated plastic parts for our model airplanes. With your opposing thumb and a good grip you could tighten bolts. You could mark measurements and have a good straightedge ruler. It hammered nails, knocked jar tops loose, banged open walnuts.

Occasionally someone would even grab it to spread jelly on muffins. Years later when a friend told me about the notion of the right tool for each task, it was a revelation. I hadn't realized we were mechanically deprived. I didn't know we were instrumentally illiterate. We thought we had most problems pretty well in hand.

After all, we had our butter knife.

UNIVERSITY

I was in the office reading term papers, chair tilted back, my feet propped against the edge of the desk. A knock at the door, and a blond, kind of heavy guy, early thirties, looking vaguely familiar, sticks his head in, smiles big, and says, "Hey, just thought I'd drop by and say hello."

It was a student who I hadn't seen in, I don't know, seven years or more, and when he said his name I remembered his quick mind and the class he was in, and some of the other people he hung out with.

He tells me what he's been doing—went to the Coast with a friend, got bit parts in cheapo horror movies, managed a fern bar, lived in Mexico, worked on a coastal steamer, got deadly ill, finally went to law school, married now with a kid.

And I thought, Here this person has been doing all this and he finds his teacher in the same position he left him seven years ago, feet on the desk, reading term papers.

I thought about what that might mean and what he might be thinking, and should I worry about it? Was I one of those characters who seem never to live, who work forty years for the firm, never looking past their green eyeshades?

What should I do? Get a ticket to Katmandu? Buy a monster truck? And then I thought, no, that my obligation was not to become a Zen Buddhist in Colorado, then do stand-up comedy in New Jersey, get interested in welding, and finally take up large-scale sculpture out of wrecked car chassis. And not to have tempestuous relationships with a historic succession of people who would break tables, wreck cars, have to be dried or bailed out at frequent intervals.

Perhaps it was my calling to do what I love—to read, write, talk about what I learned, think up theories to explain things, and keep my feet on the desk. You return to your college town; the stores you shopped in have vanished utterly, the bars you drank in have different names, the restaurants you ate in are law offices, and the houses you rented have been bulldozed.

The university itself, though, should be the one place where the trees are as green as you remember, the buildings standing just where you left them; the halls should be beige, the posters should be tattered, the classrooms vaguely grimy. The students scraggly, scruffy, smooth, or sleek, but doing the same things, hanging out, talking on the steps, yelling from cars.

And when you come to a familiar office door you should be able to knock, and have someone look up at you from a desk littered with what looks like what was on it when you left several lifetimes ago, and that person should tilt his head back and say hello in that voice that meant something to you back then.

And you can feel the pleasure that might come from staying in one place to think, to learn, to pass on what meant something to you a long time ago, and what you came back to find.

SMOKING

When cigarettes come up in conversation, people tell their stories. Victories, defeats. They ask me if I ever smoked. Yes and no, I say. When I was in tenth grade I was determined to be attractive to the girls in my school. That was a problem, since their conversation suggested they were all dating Marines stationed at Parris Island, or college men who were invariably premed, or local boys with multiple tattoos. Some would have snapshots of themselves with sailors and the Coney Island ferris wheel behind them. The ones dating college students were always knitting argyle socks.

I was invisible.

It struck me that smoking might be the answer. Tough guys

smoked, older guys smoked, intense intellectuals smoked. I watched the suavest guys in our high school. I wanted to do this right. I tried to figure out what brand would fit the personality I was trying to invent for myself. I was not a Camels kind of person. I feared I would look like my friend Sidney, who bought a black leather motorcycle jacket to make him appear dangerous on the way to his violin lessons.

I thought I ought to go for something sophisticated, Continental. And though I was neither in the Marines nor at Harvard, I was somewhere else, somewhere vaguely mysterious, alienated, alluring.

I found a cigarette called Regents. They came in a flat box with an overwrap of gold foil. I imagined sloe-eyed young women expressing wonder at my audacity and taste for discovering these elegant objects. I had embarked on the life of the smoker.

Learning to smoke was not easy. Criticism was fierce. Guys would accuse each other of not really inhaling, of holding the cigarette wrong. I figured out how not to get it wet when I had to put it between my lips. I worked on striking matches without setting the book on fire, not lighting the cigarette an inch from the tip, not flicking ashes on my own pants.

I took my cigarettes to the community center where we hung out. I flashed my Regents with a sense of making the move that was going to establish me as dangerous and interesting.

But in trying simultaneously to smoke and be charming, I

discovered a fatal flaw. No matter what I did, somehow the tendrils of smoke found their way to my tender retinas. Tears would run down my cheeks. Witty conversation, dashing demeanor is impossible when you're crying. I never finished my first pack of Regents.

Now, when I see others brandishing their Tiparillos and Marlboro Lights, I am not smug. I was saved from the life of a smoker by neither will nor foresight, but by my own miraculous incompetence.

BREAD CRUMBS

I rise at six-thirty a.m. and walk my puzzled dogs. Isn't it too early? Isn't it dark? Are you going to do something to us?

I explain I have to leave early to drive three hours for an appointment to see what the doctor in the research hospital thinks about my local chemotherapy, my high-tech radiotherapy, my recovering body.

I drive the interstate through forests and farms of blooming wild crabapple trees, brilliant redbuds, and white plum blossoms. Lately I notice I am more sensitive to symbolism. A few days ago at the end of a dinner at a Chinese restaurant, my fortune cookie was empty. I couldn't sleep that night. I choose to take this flowering landscape as a good sign, a celebration of renewed life punctuated by random sneezes.

Jerome Stern

I leave the highway and head toward the hospital through a campus of students crossing streets in thick traffic, clearly oblivious to their own mortality. I navigate by memory. It feels like I've gone far enough, it feels like I should turn right, it feels like I need to go back a block, okay, here it is. My last visit said they were doing the right thing. I carefully park in the same parking space.

In the waiting room, I read a gift catalog that tells me I can grow my own mushrooms at home. I can buy a raku ocarina. I'm not sure if there is a message in that for me.

My name is called by a muscular redheaded man who doesn't move like anyone who works indoors with medical instruments and sick people. He looks as if he's more accustomed to operating backhoes or leaning against the walls of pool halls. He says to come with him to get my blood pressure, pulse, and temperature measured. I sit down in a little room and note that the digital reading on the machine shows the person who preceded me had blood pressure of 89 over 33. I don't want to know how to interpret that.

The redheaded man has a tattoo on each finger which I make out as AMAY, but which maybe had meant to read AWAY. I can't see his other hand. Maybe it says KEEP. He goes smoothly from thermometer to cuffing my arm, talking amiably about how the guys tease him about his ponytail. He makes me feel relaxed, like he is doing his job fine, and I am being part of his rehabilitation. Perhaps another good sign.

Life lately has felt like a dark fairy tale. I am under a spell.

I am trying to have it lifted. When I was little I always thought if people in fairy tales read fairy tales they would know that they should give bread to beggars, lift withered crones who had fallen into muddy ditches, help mice in distress.

I tell the nurse who takes my blood that she is really gentle and I had hardly felt it, which is true, and she says thank you with much feeling, and modestly adds that she gets a lot of practice.

The doctor himself magically appears, and adjusts himself to me, this patient, this problem to solve, and then goes off with months of my charts and scans and evaluations and reports— the wizard who knows what he knows and knows what he does not know and what he should not say and what he might say. He is gone for a while. I do not know what to think. This business of reading signs can wear you out.

He returns to chat amiably. He notes I have responded well to the elixirs and potions. The latest readings from my interior are, in medicine's wonderfully understated language, "unremarkable." Not unremarkable to me, I think.

The doctor tells me there is nothing more to do now except resume doing whatever I do. Problems could return, or could not. There are risks, surprises, eventualities, inevitabilities. I am understanding, yes, I still could unearth a pot of gold, or I might be eaten by a wolf, or I may simply follow the bread crumbs back to a warm hearth and my sleepy dogs.

It sounds just like life.

SPRING

Every spring I ask my friend the names of the flowers, and every spring I have to learn them all over again. He explains, "The yellow vine is Jasmine. The red bush is Quince."

Every spring I have to ask my friend which is the Peach, the Plum, the Pear, and the Cherry. Are those Snowdrops? Is that Redbud? This has made me reflect on the evolution of humans. The thousands of years in which I have said, "Did you notice the days keep getting warmer? What's happening? Are we going to be cooked?"

And my good friend, the same good friend who tells me about the flowers, will say, "Don't you remember this happened the last year the same way? The sun got hotter. The days grew longer. It happened just the same way."

"Gee," I say. "What do you call it?"

"Spring," he says. "It is a season." I dimly recall him telling me that last year. I have to remember it this time. Spring.

This goes on for centuries.

It's the human condition. We start out being able to remember things that happen every day. For example, at night we don't panic because the air is turning black. We remember from yesterday. It did the same thing. It stayed black for a while and you can't hunt or fish, and then the blackness goes away.

But what about things that happen once a year, like the return of the myrtle warblers? Or once every four years, like the election of a president? Or every several years, like marriages and divorces and inflations, and recessions, and wars?

Humans have a very hard time remembering what happened the last time. They don't recognize what it looks like as it approaches. They don't remember how it felt. They can't recall what they're supposed to do. And if they don't have a friend to remind them, they might be in serious trouble.

BOOKLOVE

I have just come from an exhibition that told me that books will be replaced by electronic libraries, talking videos, interactive computers, CD-ROMS with thousands of volumes, gigabytes of memory dancing on pixilated screens at which we will stare blearily into eternity.

And so, in the face of the future, I must sing the song of the book, for nothing more voluptuous do I know than sitting with bright pictures, fat upon my lap, and turning glossy pages of giraffes and Gauguins, penguins and pyramids. I love wide atlases delineating the rise and fall of empires, the trade routes from Kashmir to Samarkand.

I love heavy dictionaries, their tiny pictures, complicated

columns, minute definitions of incarnative and laniary, hagboat and flapdoodle. I love the texture of the pages, the high-gloss slickness of magazines as slippery as coiled eels, the soft nubble of old books, delicate India paper, so thin my hands tremble to turn the fluttering dry leaves, and the yellow cheap coarse paper of mystery novels so gripping I don't care that the plane circles Atlanta forever, because it is a full moon and I am stalking in the Arizona desert a malevolent shape-shifter.

I love the feel of ink on the paper, the shiny varnishes, the silky lacquers, the satiny mattes. I love the press of letter in thick paper, the roughness sizzles my fingers with centuries of craft embedded in pulped old rags, my hands caress the leather of old bindings crumbling like ancient gentlemen. The books I hold for their heft, to riff their pages, to smell their smoky dustiness, the rise of time in my nostrils.

I love bookstores, a perfect madness of opportunity, a lavish feast eaten by walking up aisles, and as fast as my hand reaches out, I reveal books' intimate innards, a doleful engraving of Charlotte Corday, who murdered Marat, a drawing of the 1914 T-head Stutz Bearcat, whose owners shouted at rivals, "There never was a car worser than the Mercer."

I sing these pleasures of white paper and black ink, of the small jab of the hard-cover corner at the edge of my diaphragm, of the look of type, of the flip of a page, the sinful abandon of the turned-down corner, the reckless possessiveness of my marginal scrawl, the cover picture—as much a part of the book as the contents itself, like Holden Caulfield with his red cap turned backwards, staring away from us, at what we all thought we should become.

And I also love those great fat Bibles evangelists wave like otter pelts, the long graying sets of unreadable authors, the tall books of babyhood enthusiastically crayoned, the embossed covers of adolescence, the tiny poetry anthologies you could slip in your pocket, and the yellowing cookbooks of recipes for *glace blanche* Dupont and Argentina mocha toast, their stains and spots souvenirs of long evenings full of love and argument, and the talk, like as not, of books, books, books.